Arizona

GREETINGS from

ARIZONA

THE GRAND CANYON STATE

Jim Ollhoff

Visit us at
www.abdopublishing.com

Published by ABDO Publishing Company, 8000 West 78th Street, Suite 310, Edina, Minnesota 55439 USA. Copyright ©2010 by Abdo Consulting Group, Inc. International copyrights reserved in all countries. No part of this book may be reproduced in any form without written permission from the publisher. The Checkerboard Library™ is a trademark and logo of ABDO Publishing Company.

Printed in the United States.

Editor: John Hamilton
Graphic Design: Sue Hamilton
Cover Illustration: Neil Klinepier
Cover Photo: iStock Photo

Manufactured with paper containing at least 10% post-consumer waste

Interior Photo Credits: Alamy, AP Images, Arizona Cardinals, Arizona Coyotes, Arizona Diamondbacks, Comstock, Corbis, David Olson, Getty, Granger Collection, iStock Photo, Library of Congress, Lu Giddings, Mike Lakers, Mile High Maps, Mountain High Maps, National Archives, North Wind Picture Archives, One Mile Up, Peter Arnold Inc, Phoenix Mercury, Phoenix Suns, U.S. Congress, and the U.S. States Postal Service.
Statistics: State population statistics taken from 2008 U.S. Census Bureau estimates. City and town population statistics taken from July 1, 2007, U.S. Census Bureau estimates. Land and water area statistics taken from 2000 Census, U.S. Census Bureau.

Library of Congress Cataloging-in-Publication Data

Ollhoff, Jim, 1959-
  Arizona / Jim Ollhoff.
     p. cm. -- (The United States)
  Includes index.
  ISBN 978-1-60453-638-6
  1. Arizona--Juvenile literature. I. Title.

F811.3.O455 2010
979.1--dc22
                        2008051000

Table of Contents

Grand Canyon State

   Arizona is a land of stark desert beauty. The famous Grand Canyon is one of many national parks, national monuments, and national historic landmarks in the state.

   When Arizona was first set up, its leaders came up with many reasons why people should move to the state. They said Arizona had five C's: copper, cattle, cotton, citrus, and climate. Copper was heavily mined in Arizona. Many cattle were raised in the state. Farmers grew cotton and citrus fruits. The climate was clean and dry, which people believed would cure many sicknesses.

   The five C's worked. Whether people came for mining, farming, or clean air, they found Arizona to be a good place to live.

Arizona's Grand Canyon
National Park at sunset.

Quick Facts

Name: Arizona is possibly a Basque (people living in Northern Spain) word meaning "The Good Oak Tree," or a Native American word that means "small spring."

State Capital: Phoenix

Date of Statehood: February 14, 1912 (48th state)

Population: 6,500,180 (14th-most populous state)

Area (Total Land and Water): 113,998 square miles (295,253 sq km), 6th-largest state

Largest City: Phoenix, population 1,552,259

Nickname: The Grand Canyon State

Motto: *Ditat Deus* (God Enriches)

State Bird: Cactus Wren

State Flower: White Blossom of the Saguaro Cactus

State Gem: Turquoise

State Tree: Palo Verde

State Song: "Arizona March Song" and "Arizona"

Highest Point: Humphreys Peak, 12,633 feet (3,851 m)

Lowest Point: Colorado River, 70 feet (22 m)

Average July Temperature: 97°F (36°C)

Record High Temperature: 128°F (53°C), June 29, 1994, Lake Havasu

Average January Temperature: 65°F (18°C)

Record Low Temperature: -40°F (-40°C), January 7, 1971, Hawley Lake

Humphreys Peak

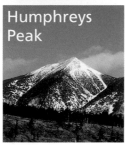

Average Annual Precipitation: 13 inches (33 cm)

Number of U.S. Senators: 2

Number of U.S. Representatives: 8

U.S. Postal Service Abbreviation: AZ

Geography

Arizona is the sixth-largest state in the Union. Nevada and California border Arizona to the west. On the east side is New Mexico. Utah is to the north, and the Mexican state of Sonora is to its south.

There are 20 Native American reservations in the state. The largest is for the Navajo and Hopi tribes. Native American culture plays a big part of life in Arizona.

Much of Arizona is desert. Cactus, creosote, and other desert plants live in the hot, dry conditions. Arizona also has one of the largest stands of evergreen ponderosa pine trees in the world.

Mountains and plateaus dot the state. Arizona has many scenic national parks, national monuments, and historic trails.

Arizona's total land and water area is 113,998 square miles (295,253 sq km). It is the 6th-largest state. The state capital is Phoenix.

The Grand Canyon is probably the state's most famous landmark. Located in the northern part of the state, this deep gorge was cut by the Colorado River over millions of years. The canyon's width ranges from about 0.1 to 18 miles (0.2 to 29 km). It winds its way across 277 miles (446 km). In places, it is more than a mile (1.6 km) deep.

A donkey stands overlooking the Grand Canyon. Many visitors ride the sturdy animals down into the canyon.

Barringer Meteor Crater.

One of our planet's biggest meteor craters sits near the center of the state. A meteor is a rock traveling through space. When Earth's gravity catches it, the rock turns into a meteorite that falls, crashing forcefully into the ground. Arizona's Barringer Meteor Crater is a gigantic hole left by a long-ago meteorite. The crater is almost 1 mile (1.6 km) wide and 570 feet (174 m) deep.

Climate and Weather

Most of Arizona is arid, which means it is very dry. Though some areas in the mountains can get 25 inches (64 cm) of rain per year, most areas get half that amount.

Much of Arizona is arid.

The southern part of Arizona is largely desert. The winters are mild and the summers are very hot. In the summer, the temperature can be 90° to 120° Fahrenheit (32°–48°C). Because the air is dry, there are big swings in temperature. At night in the summer, it can drop 50° Fahrenheit (28°C).

The northern part of Arizona is higher in elevation. This makes the climate cooler. During winter, temperatures can sometimes go below 0° Fahrenheit (-18°C).

In the summer, there is a monsoon season. A monsoon is a wind that lasts a long time, even for weeks or months. From mid-July to August, the monsoons can bring fierce thunderstorms.

Fierce thunderstorms fill the Arizona sky with bolts of lightning.

Plants and Animals

Much of Arizona is desert. About a quarter of Arizona is forested. Another quarter of Arizona is grassland.

In the high elevations, the forests have many kinds of trees. These include the ponderosa pine, Douglas fir, spruces, and aspen. Black bears, deer, antelope, and elk are found in the mountains, but can be found elsewhere as well.

In the desert areas, there are many different types of cactus. Cacti store water, saving it for the hot, dry months when little or no rain falls. Mesquite trees are also common. Mesquite trees have very long roots that reach down to find deep underground water. Saltbush and sagebrush are common shrubs.

A bear cub in a pine tree. Bears are found in Arizona's mountain areas.

Desert reptiles include rattlesnakes, Arizona coral snakes, and Gila monsters. Bobcats, coyotes, and mountain lions can be found across the state. Small animals include porcupines, skunks, foxes, and collared peccaries (sometimes called javelinas or wild pigs).

Birds are plentiful in the southern part of the state. Game birds include turkeys, quail, and doves.

A saguaro cactus blooms.

In the rivers, the Colorado squawfish is common. The Apache trout is the official fish of Arizona.

The state flower is the white blossom of the saguaro cactus. The fragrant blooms appear in May and June.

Mountain lions are found throughout Arizona.

Gila Monster

Rattlesnake

Collared Peccary

History

People called Paleo-Indians lived in Arizona, perhaps 10,000 or 20,000 years ago. They were the ancestors of the Native Americans.

Before the Europeans, the Apache and Navajo tribes lived in Arizona. They probably arrived between 1100 and 1500 AD. The Hopi also made Arizona their home.

In the early 1500s, the Spaniards heard stories about "El Dorado." It was said to be a city made completely of gold. The story was told enough to make people believe that this city of gold really existed.

In 1539, an explorer named Marcos de Niza left Mexico City searching for this place of amazing riches. He traveled through Arizona. When he returned to Mexico, he claimed to have seen cities of gold in the distance.

In 1540-42, Francisco Vazquez de Coronado led a group of people into Arizona. There were several hundred people with him. The group explored Arizona, and even made it as far north as Kansas. To his great disappointment, Coronado did not find El Dorado. There was no city of gold to find.

From 1540-1542, Coronado searched for the golden city of El Dorado.

An Apache defends his homeland, shooting at a covered wagon.

In the next 250 years, Arizona was visited by priests, trappers, and missionaries. But the Apaches aggressively defended their homeland, so no large towns sprang up.

In 1846 to 1848, the United States fought a war with Mexico. When the United States won, they forced Mexico to give up a large area of land, including California, Nevada, Utah, most of Arizona, and parts of Texas, Colorado, and Wyoming. In 1853, the United States bought the remaining part of Arizona, the area south of Phoenix.

Soon, settlements and mining began. Copper was discovered. The new field of electrical engineering created a big demand for copper. In the 1870s, Mormons from Utah came to settle in Arizona. The U.S. Army set up forts to protect people who were traveling to California.

An Arizona copper mine in 1909.

A train in Arizona in 1903.

The railroads arrived in the 1880s. A railroad on the north side of the state connected St. Louis, Missouri, and California. A railroad in the south connected New Orleans, Louisiana, and Los Angeles, California. More communities sprang up near the railroads.

Arizona was sometimes a wild place. Miners could strike it rich or lose everything. Sheep farmers and cattlemen fought over the use of water. In some places, a town sprang up before the law would arrive. By the end of the 1880s, federal marshals and town sheriffs restored law and order to most areas.

In 1912, President Taft signed the act that made Arizona the 48th state in the Union.

On February 14, 1912, Arizona became the 48th state. Only Alaska and Hawaii joined the Union after that.

During World War II, military bases sprang up across Arizona. Prisoner-of-war camps opened, holding German, Italian, and Japanese prisoners.

After World War II, the invention of air conditioning made Arizona more livable. The state became very popular with retirees. Today, many retired people from northern states live in Arizona during the winter months. Arizona residents call these people "snowbirds."

Did You Know?

During World War II, Navajo soldiers known as code talkers used their Native American language to send radio messages to other military units.

In 1942, shortly after the United States entered World War II, it was discovered that the enemy often intercepted American military radio messages. The messages, often action plans, were coded. The problem was that the Japanese were good at decoding messages. The United States needed a better code.

It was discovered that the Native American Navajo tribe had one of the most difficult languages on earth. Only a few people knew how to speak it. The U.S. Marine Corps recruited 29 Navajo speakers, and spread them out in military units.

Navajo **code** talkers operate a portable **radio** set in 1943.

The code talkers spoke to each other over the radio. They used some Navajo words for letters and some for common military terms. For example, the word hummingbird meant "fighter plane." The Navajo word for it was "da-he-tih-hi." The code was so successful that more than 300 additional Navajos were recruited to join the service.

After the war, Japanese generals admitted that the only code they couldn't break was the Navajo code. In recent years, the Navajo code talkers have been honored for their work by the United States.

People

Senator **John McCain**
(1936-) was born at Coco
Solo Naval Air Station
in the Panama Canal
Zone. His father and his
grandfather were both

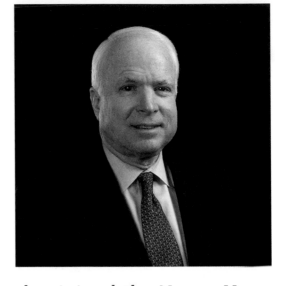

U.S. Navy admirals. McCain also joined the Navy. He
was a pilot in the Vietnam War. In 1967, his plane
was shot down. He survived more than five years as
a prisoner-of-war. In 1973, he was finally released.
He earned many medals, including the Silver Star and
Purple Heart. In 1981, he moved to Phoenix, and began
working in politics. In 1986, McCain was elected to the
U.S. Senate. He has served as an Arizona senator since.
In 2008, he made an unsuccessful run for president.

Cochise (1815?–1874) was a chief of the Apache Native American tribe. In the 1860s, he led his people as they defended their Apache homeland. In 1861, the U.S. Army accused him and other tribe members of a crime they didn't commit. Some Apaches were killed, but Cochise escaped. He led a fierce and often violent fight against white settlements on Apache land. He surrendered in 1872, and went to live on an Arizona reservation. Cochise died two years later. A county in Arizona and a college in the state are named after him.

Sandra Day O'Connor

(1930-) was born in Texas, but grew up on a ranch near Duncan, Arizona. She graduated near the top of her law school class in 1952. However, because she was a woman, she couldn't get a job with a law firm. So, she worked as a county attorney. O'Connor was elected to the Arizona Senate in 1969. She became a judge in Maricopa County, near Phoenix. Later, she was appointed to the Arizona Court of Appeals. She was appointed to the Supreme Court of the United States in 1981. She was the first woman to serve on the Supreme Court. She retired from that position in 2006.

Astronomer **Percival Lowell** (1855–1916) went to school at Harvard University. In 1894 he moved to Arizona and built an observatory in Flagstaff. In the early 1900s, he watched planet Neptune's orbit. Because Neptune didn't follow the orbit that he predicted, Lowell thought there was another planet farther out. He called it "Planet X" and tried to find it with his telescope. Pluto was discovered in 1930 using Lowell's telescope.

Wyatt Earp (1848-1929) was a lawman, gambler, businessman, treasure-seeker, and many other things. In 1879 he moved to Tombstone, Arizona. Wyatt Earp, along with two of his brothers, and friend Doc Holliday, got into a feud with an outlaw group led by Ike Clanton. In 1881, their shoot-out near Tombstone's O.K. Corral became famous.

Cities

Phoenix was founded in 1868 by people looking for a good place to farm. Ruins from a Native American settlement showed where canals could be built to bring in water. The town was built. It soon became a railroad stop. Today, the population of Phoenix itself is 1,552,259. However, the whole metropolitan area numbers more than four million people. Phoenix is the state's largest city, as well as its capital. Arizona State University is one of several colleges in the area.

Tucson is the second-largest city in Arizona, with a population of 525,529. Europeans first visited the area in the 1690s. The Spanish built a fort in the area in 1775. It came to be known as Tucson, a Pima Native American word for "spring at the foot of a black mountain." The University of Arizona is located in Tucson. The university and military bases provide many jobs for the people of the city.

Flagstaff was first settled in 1876. Nestled near huge pine forests, the lumber industry quickly became an important part of the town's economy. Flagstaff became a stop for the early railroads. Northern Arizona University and Coconino Community College are located in Flagstaff. Lowell Observatory is located there also. Astronomers at the Lowell Observatory discovered the dwarf planet Pluto in 1930. Flagstaff has a population of 59,746.

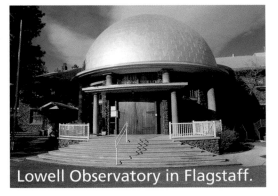

Lowell Observatory in Flagstaff.

Tombstone was one of the most well known of the early mining camps. Ed Schieffelin came to the area in 1877, looking for gold. His friends told him he'd be finding his tombstone, rather than wealth. Proving his friends wrong, Schieffelin found silver and became rich. Ed named his mining claim "Tombstone," and the name passed on to the city when it was founded. The famous shoot-out near the O.K. Corral was in Tombstone. Today, with a population of 1,562, the town is a popular place for tourists to visit.

Main Street in Tombstone, Arizona.

Transportation

Many of today's roads follow former wagon train roads. These roads followed pioneer trails, which followed the earlier Native American trade

A morning train leaves Flagstaff.

routes. Railroads came through Arizona in the 1880s. Passenger trains still travel through the state today.

The main interstate highways are I-40, I-8, and I-10. Each travels east and west. Interstates 19 and 17 run north and south. Interstate 15 cuts across the very northwest corner of the state. There are many other roads and highways across Arizona.

The biggest airport in Arizona is Phoenix Sky Harbor International Airport. It is one of the busiest airports in the world. Tucson International Airport is also a large facility that serves many foreign passengers. There are nearly 100 airports and airfields in Arizona.

Phoenix's Sky Harbor International Airport.

Natural Resources

A miner uses a jack leg drill.

Copper, zinc, uranium, and coal are important natural resources in Arizona. Mining is important to the state. A limited amount of oil comes from the northeast corner of Arizona.

Cotton is a major crop grown in Arizona. Alfalfa, vegetables, and nuts are grown also. Citrus fruits and grapes are important to the state.

Cattle and poultry are big sources of income as well. Arizona's average-sized farm is larger than any other state's average farm.

However, water usage is a major issue in the dry Arizona lands. Farmers and ranchers need more water as they grow their businesses. There is little groundwater in Arizona. Several states want water from the Colorado River. Many water disagreements between California and Arizona have been taken to court.

A Hopi farmer shows his stunted corn. Needed irrigation water has been used by a coal mining company.

Industry

Copper mining was one of the first industries in Arizona. Between 1880 and 1950, it was the most important industry. In fact, the Arizona state

A large copper mining operation in Morenci, Arizona.

flag has a copper star in the middle to remind people of the importance of copper.

Although copper production is still important, the state has several other major industries. Electronics, computer software, communications, and engineering bring money to the state. The state government is the largest employer.

Tourism has become important to the economy as well. A large number of retired people from northern states live in Arizona in the winter. Arizona has many national parks and national monuments. The most famous of these is the Grand Canyon.

Tourists enjoy meeting an Arizona prospector and his horses.

Sports

The Cardinals, Coyotes, Diamondbacks, Suns, and Mercury are some of Arizona's professional sports teams.

There are a number of professional sports teams in Arizona. The Arizona Cardinals are part of the National Football League. The Phoenix Coyotes play in the National Hockey League. The Arizona Diamondbacks are a Major League Baseball team. The Phoenix Suns are members of the National Basketball Association. The Phoenix Mercury play in the Women's National Basketball Association.

Arizona also has minor league teams, such as the Yuma Scorpions baseball team. Another sports team is the Arizona Rattlers. They play arena football.

There are many college sports, too. The University of Arizona Wildcats and the Arizona State Sun Devils are rivals. The teams play great games against each other.

Arizona has several beautiful golf courses, which attract golfers of all skill levels to the state.

There are many outdoor activities. Arizona has more national parks and national monuments than any other state. The different terrains offer adventures to campers, hikers, bikers, hunters, and more.

Hiking, mountain biking, camping, hunting, and river rafting are just some of the sports enjoyed in Arizona.

Entertainment

Arizona is a popular place to film movies and television shows. Hollywood filmmakers have made many movies in the state, including westerns and science fiction pictures. Arizona is the home of many musical groups as well.

Native American art is found all over Arizona. Hopi and Navajo artists produce all types of beautiful artwork including paintings, jewelry, blankets, and pottery.

Beautiful Native American jewelry, blankets, and pottery.

The San Xavier del Bac Mission is called the "White Dove of the Desert." Construction of the buildings began in 1783. Rising out of the desert, the mission can be seen for miles.

Many buildings are designed in a Spanish style. This reflects the history of the state. The San Xavier del Bac Mission near Tucson was completed in 1797. Sometimes called the "White Dove of the Desert," it is one of the most photographed buildings in the state.

Phoenix and Tucson have active theater companies and performing arts. Museums and art collections show the artwork and history of the many cultures in Arizona.

Timeline

1100-1500—Apache, Hopi, and Navajo tribes live in the area that will become Arizona.

1539—Marcos de Niza explores the area, looking for gold.

1540-1542—Francisco Vazquez de Coronado leads a group of people into Arizona, exploring the state and looking for El Dorado, the city of gold.

1846-1848—The Mexican-American War is fought. The United States takes over ownership of land that will become Arizona.

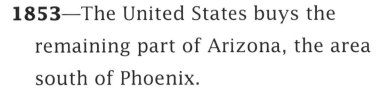**1853**—The United States buys the remaining part of Arizona, the area south of Phoenix.

**1854**—Copper is discovered in Arizona.

1863—Arizona becomes a territory of the United States.

**1912**—Arizona becomes the 48th state.

**1919**—The Grand Canyon becomes Arizona's first national park.

**1942-1945**—Navajo code talkers serve with the U.S. Marines in World War II.

2001—The Arizona Diamondbacks baseball team wins the World Series.

Glossary

Apache—A Native American tribe that lived in Arizona before the Europeans arrived. They fiercely fought to defend and keep their homeland from white settlers.

Arid—A very dry climate.

El Dorado—A fabled city made completely of gold. Some early Spanish explorers believed the city existed in what is today the southwestern United States.

Hopi—A Native American tribe that lived in Arizona before the Europeans arrived.

Marcos de Niza—A Spanish explorer who traveled through the Arizona area in 1539.

Monsoon—A wind that lasts a long time, even for weeks or months. Summer months are monsoon season in Arizona.

Navajo—A group of Native Americans that live primarily in Arizona, New Mexico, and Utah. They are known for their work with livestock, as well as creating beautiful weavings, pottery, and silver jewelry.

Paleo-Indians—People who lived very early in North and South America. These people are believed to be the ancestors of the Native Americans.

Plateau—An area of high ground that is mostly flat at the top.

Snowbirds—People from northern states who come to Arizona during the winter months.

Vietnam War—A conflict between the countries of North Vietnam and South Vietnam from 1954-1975. Communist North Vietnam was supported by China and the Soviet Union. The United States entered the war on the side of South Vietnam.

World War II—A conflict across the world, lasting from 1939-1945. The United States entered the war in December of 1941.

Index